For Flea

First published 2007 by Walker Books Ltd
87 Vauxhall Walk, London SE11 5HJ

2 4 6 8 10 9 7 5 3 1

© 2007 Penny Dale

The right of Penny Dale to be identified as author/illustrator
of this work has been asserted by her in accordance with the
Copyright, Designs and Patents Act 1988

This book has been typeset in Usherwood

Printed in China

British Library Cataloguing in Publication Data:
a catalogue record for this book is available from the British Library

ISBN 978-1-4063-0147-2

www.walkerbooks.co.uk

The BOY ON the BUS

Penny Dale

BUS STOP

WALKER BOOKS
AND SUBSIDIARIES
LONDON · BOSTON · SYDNEY · AUCKLAND

The boy on the bus drives
round and round,
round and round,
round and round.
The boy on the bus drives
round and round.

Who wants to ride on the bus?

Ducks!

The boy on the bus says, "Up you come!
Tickets here! Lots of room!"

The boy on the bus says, "All aboard!
Ready, steady, go!"

The ducks on the bus go
Quack quack quack!
Quack quack quack!
Quack quack quack!
The ducks on the bus go
Quack
quack
quack!

Who wants to ride on the bus?

Pigs!

The boy on the bus says, "On you get!
Take a seat! Not full yet!"

The boy on the bus says, "All aboard!
Ready, steady, go!"

The pigs on the bus go
Oink oink oink!
Oink oink oink!
Oink oink oink!
The pigs on the bus go
Oink oink oink!
Ding-ding! Off we go!

The ducks on the bus go
Quack quack quack!
Quack quack quack!
Quack quack quack!
The ducks on the bus go
Quack
quack
quack!

Who wants to

ride on the bus?

Chickens! Goats!

The boy on the bus says, "Room inside!

Move on back! Enjoy the ride!"

The boy on the bus says, "All aboard!
Ready, steady, go!"

The cows on the bus go
Moo moo moo!
The horse on the bus goes
Neigh neigh neigh!
The chickens on the bus go
Cluck cluck cluck!
Ding-ding! Off we go!

The goats on the bus go
Bleat bleat bleat!
The pigs on the bus go
Oink oink oink!
The ducks on the bus go
Quack
            quack
                        quack!

Who wants to ride on the bus?

Sheep!

The boy on the bus says, "What a crowd!

Climb up here! Careful now!"

The boy on the bus says, "Hold on tight!
Ready, steady, go!"

The sheep on the bus go
Baa baa baa!
Baa baa baa!
Baa baa baa!
The sheep on the bus go
Baa baa baa!
Ding-ding! Off we go!

The cows on the bus go
Moo moo moo!
The horse on the bus goes
Neigh neigh neigh!
The chickens on the bus go
Cluck cluck cluck!
Ding-ding! Off we go!

The goats on the bus go
Bleat bleat bleat!
The pigs on the bus go
Oink oink oink!
The ducks on the bus go
Quack
quack
quack!

READY, STEADY, GO!

The wheels on the bus go
round and round,
round and round,
round and round.
The wheels on the bus go
round and round

Baa baa!

Baa!

Baa!

Baa baa!

Baa baa!

Baaaaaa!

Baaaaaa!

Baaaa baa!

Baa baa!

Quack!
Quack!

Mooooo!

Moooo!

Cluck cluck!

Bleat!
Bleat!

Bleeeat!

Oink oink!

Oink oink!

Quack!
Quack!

Neigh!
Neigh!

all day long!